EXTREME CAREERS

ADVENTURE TOUR GUIDES

Life on Extreme Outdoor Adventures

Chérie Turner

the rosen publishing group's
rosen central

Published in 2003 by The Rosen Publishing Group, Inc.
29 East 21st Street, New York, NY 10010

First Edition

Library of Congress Cataloging-in-Publication Data

Turner, Chérie
Adventure tour guides : life on extreme outdoor adventures / by Chérie Turner.—1st ed.
    p. cm. — (Extreme careers)
Summary: Explores how to prepare for and get into the field of adventure guiding, and looks at the daily life of those who choose to work as adventure tour guides.
Includes bibliographical references (p.   ).
ISBN 0-8239-3793-3 (lib. bdg.)
1. Tour guides (Persons)—Vocational guidance. 2. Sports and tourism—Vocational guidance. [1. Tour guides (Persons). 2. Adventure and adventurers—Vocational guidance. 3. Tourism—Vocational guidance.
4. Vocational guidance.] I. Title. II. Series.
G154.7 .T87 2002
338.4'791023'73—dc21

2002007953

Manufactured in the United States of America

Contents

Introduction

In recent years, more and more people have wanted to experience extreme outdoor adventures. But few people are able to reach the level of expertise needed to take those adventures on their own. Adventure guides make it possible for lesser-skilled people to experience extreme challenges. Beth Rypins, a world-class white-water rafting guide and kayaker, explained some of the challenges of this career in an interview: "[Adventure guides take] responsibility for people in an arena where they can't take responsibility for themselves." And nowadays there are guides for any adventure imaginable: white-water rafting, kayaking, mountaineering (climbing very large mountains), rock climbing, and ice climbing, just to name a few.

Being an adventure tour guide can involve traveling to exotic locales and engaging in sports such as ice-climbing.

Adventure Tour Guides: Life on Extreme Outdoor Adventures

The primary job of a guide is to take responsibility for another person's well-being in the unforgiving outdoors, which is a very challenging task. To do this, guides must be experts in their sport, be very physically fit, deal well with their clients and other guides, and know how to remain calm and effective in frightening situations. Though you might think that guides are daredevils to take these risks, adventure guides always consider safety first and learn to firmly say no when they feel there is a potential for disaster. But that does not mean injuries (or worse) do not sometimes happen, even to the most experienced and careful of guides. Nature is unpredictable; there is always a great level of risk involved in taking clients into these unknown situations.

There are practical questions to ask about the career of adventure guiding. How do guides get hired? How competitive is this field? What other careers is one qualified to pursue after having worked as a guide? You will learn the answers to these questions and more as we explore the challenging, rewarding, and risky career of adventure guiding.

Guiding Skills: What the Job Requires

Adventure guides are responsible for taking people into challenging and exciting outdoor situations. They are also responsible for making sure that everyone stays safe. There are two primary qualifications for being a guide: expertise in the discipline he or she is guiding and the ability to be comfortable and direct with people.

Expertise in the Field

People become guides because they have a passion for the adventurous outdoor lifestyle. Many are interested in pursuing the limits of their own abilities, such as

Having expertise in a particular field, like this woman who is rock-climbing in Utah, and being physically fit enough to use that expertise are crucial prerequisites for those who want to guide.

climbing the world's highest mountains—like Mount Everest—or kayaking remote white-water rapids. Many work as guides in order to finance these personal goals and also to share their passion with others. This passion is an important part of being a guide. Guides must first and foremost be experts in the field. They must have a lot of personal experience in the sport. For example, rock climbing guides must know how to climb very well. They need to know about all of the equipment necessary and how to use it. They must have a lot of varied climbing experience. And finally (and, for guides, most important), they must know how to assess risks and stay as safe as possible in the often harsh environment of the outdoors.

Fitness

In addition to their expertise, guides must be very physically fit. According to Beth Rypins, a good guide "has to be very capable physically." Outdoor adventures can be very strenuous. Guides not only have to complete the adventure themselves, they also have to help their clients. On a river, this may mean that a guide must negotiate white water while pulling a fallen client back into the raft. Or, in a mountaineering situation, a guide may need to assist a client who is incapable of getting to the safety of camp on his or her own power. Guides are often also responsible for hauling equipment, setting up camp, and doing any number of other physically taxing jobs to keep the trip running smoothly. This all adds up to long, physically demanding days. Good physical fitness is crucial for a career as an adventure tour guide.

A good amount of endurance is required of guides so that they can handle the physically taxing aspects of guiding.

Staying Safe

There is always the potential for disaster when pursuing outdoor adventures. The first responsibility of a guide is to keep people as safe as possible. This is always the number one priority for any guide. Consequently, it is critical that a guide knows how to assess risks and make decisions that will prevent disaster. A guide must also be trained to respond to emergency situations in the event that an accident does occur.

All guides must be trained in advanced first aid and CPR (cardiopulmonary resuscitation—an emergency procedure to help someone who has stopped breathing). There are also a number of outdoor-specific emergency medical certifications, such as Wilderness First Responder (WFR) and Wilderness Emergency Medical Technician (WEMT), which are very useful and necessary for those who guide the most extreme adventures.

Additionally, a guide should have specific training for his or her particular sport. Mountaineering guides should have avalanche training and should understand and be able to deal with altitude sickness. Whitewater rafting and kayaking guides should be trained in

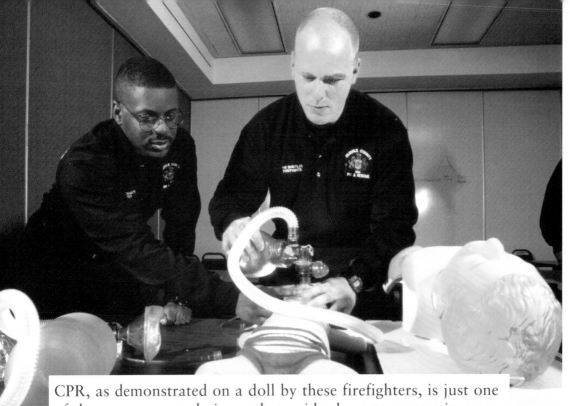

CPR, as demonstrated on a doll by these firefighters, is just one of the emergency techniques that guides have to master in case an emergency occurs on their watch.

swift-water rescue, which includes rescue techniques for rapidly moving water.

Also helpful, but not absolutely necessary, is experience as an emergency medical technician (EMT), firefighter, or any other job that deals with emergency rescue.

A guide needs to be able to respond effectively and capably to emergency situations, and training ensures that he or she has the tools to do so. Even guides who have years of experience must keep their skills honed.

In an interview, professional mountaineer and guide Kathryn Hess of Jackson Hole Mountain Guides in Jackson, Wyoming, noted that safety training is an integral part of preparing for each upcoming guiding season: "We train at the beginning of the season in high angle rescue for the times when prevention doesn't work. We keep up on the latest techniques and buy the latest gear. We educate ourselves all in the name of prevention and rescue."

Mental Strength and Patience

Guiding is as much a mental challenge as it is a physical challenge. The physical demands of the adventure alone require a great deal of mental strength. When faced with the unpredictability of nature, a guide needs to remain focused and make quick, confident decisions. And the days are often long and exhausting. A guide needs to be able to maintain a confident and unwavering attitude regardless of such fatigue.

There is also the added factor of dealing with clients. When asked what makes a good guide, Hess's first response was: "Patience!" Indeed, patience is a critical component of being able to deal well with clients, especially those who are difficult and demanding. Also, clients rely heavily on a guide's expertise to get through dangerous situations. The stress of this responsibility can be mentally taxing. In the face of it all, a guide needs to remain calm, positive, and assuring.

Ability to Work Well with Clients

A guide's job is to help a client achieve success— scale the rock, run the river, reach the top of the mountain—while experiencing as little risk as possible. Remember, safety is always the highest priority on any guided adventure. The guide is also responsible for making sure that clients are well cared for and are having an enjoyable time. A guide needs "to help a client feel at ease and comfortable in uncomfortable situations," said Kathryn Hess. And Beth Rypins noted: "[Clients] are coming into an environment that isn't theirs so it's really good as a guide if you can make people welcome."

Patience is a very important virtue when dealing with clients, especially while teaching them emergency techniques. Here, students take part in avalanche rescue training at the Outward Bound School, a New York–based outdoor training program.

The following are some key skills guides need to be able to successfully handle clients.

Assessing Ability

One of the most important aspects of dealing with a client is being able to assess his or her ability. If the guide understands a client's physical and mental abilities, the guide can push the client to his or her limits while keeping everyone safe. "As a guide, that's the first thing I do," said Rypins. "I assess someone's ability. I assess their physical fitness level, their mental fitness level. I assess how comfortable they are in the group . . . It took years to develop this [ability to assess people], and it took some really big mistakes. I had to trust my judgment."

Safety First: Learning to Say No

Clients pay to be taken out for a challenging and adventurous experience. It is the guide's job to ensure that this happens for everyone. Most times clients and guides work as a group in extreme situations to reach the intended goal. But one client's lack of ability can cause everyone to be put in great danger. Again, it's a guide's primary responsibility to make sure that everyone is as safe as possible and that risks are limited. Sometimes this means that, after assessing everyone's ability levels, a guide must tell one or more clients that they cannot complete the adventure. "It's my job to let them [the clients] know that not everyone gets to go on Class V [the most difficult white-water sections of a river]," according to Rypins. This is an extremely difficult but important task. Clients don't like to be told that they are not even allowed to attempt the adventure they have come to face, but that decision can be the difference between success and disaster for all involved.

Knowledge of the Area

Guiding isn't only about the adventure; it's also about experiencing a new and beautiful environment. Learning about and sharing information with clients about the history, geology, and/or plant and wildlife of the area adds to the experience and makes it more enjoyable. For example, a guide who is leading trips through the Grand Canyon should know and be able to explain how the canyon was formed. A guide who is taking clients to another country should know about the culture and the history of the people and the area. It is also very helpful to be able to speak the language that is spoken in the area where one is guiding.

The Guiding Personality

Guides continually work with new and different people. It is therefore very helpful if guides are out-going and sociable so that they are able to deal well with a wide variety of personalities. Also, outdoor adventures can be tough. Just living in nature is uncomfortable for most people. Mornings and evenings can be cold. Showers are icy or nonexistent. Cooking is laborious. Rain may fall or strong winds may blow. Now add to that the discomforts of the adventure. Mountaineers start summit days in the middle of the night in freezing temperatures. White-water rafting is often done on icy cold rivers. The combination of these factors is likely to cause any client to have moments of irritability, doubt, or depression. A guide needs to

Students of the National Outdoor Leadership School (NOLS) take in the breathtaking beauty of the Chugach Mountains in Alaska. Guides learn to take hardships like fatigue and harsh weather in stride.

remain enthusiastic, patient, and upbeat to help keep clients motivated and confident.

Guides are responsible for making the adventure as comfortable and pleasant as possible. Their duties may include setting up camp, getting all necessary permits, providing and transporting equipment, supplying food, cooking, making travel reservations, or any number of other details that will allow the client to participate in an adventure with as few hassles as possible. Being able to attend to these details while also remaining pleasant and enjoyable is a very important part of being a good guide.

Two Important Factors

Guiding extreme adventures requires a wide variety of skills, many of which take years to develop and master. It is critical that a guide learn these skills because the safety of other human beings depends on the guide's ability. At the heart of good guiding, though, there are two factors that cannot be learned in any course. As Dr. Pat Tierney, rafting guide and co-owner of Adrift Adventures, simply stated: "[Guides] must have a love of the outdoors and a love of people."

The Business of Guiding

2

In addition to having the skills needed to guide in the outdoors, an adventure tour guide must know about the business side of guiding. A guide needs to know where to get training, how to find a job, how much he or she should expect to get paid, and more.

The guiding business exists within the larger outdoor adventure and sports industry. This industry is full of people who make a living exploring and preserving nature, and providing products that make outdoor adventure possible and safe. For those who want to make a career of taking clients on the most extreme outdoor challenges in the world, building a solid reputation within the outdoor adventure industry as a trustworthy, safe, and competent guide is a must.

Due to an ever-increasing interest in outdoor adventures over the last several years, opportunities in guiding have become plentiful for those who are qualified. Learning about and developing one's skills can turn a passion for sharing adventure into a life-long career.

Getting a Job as a Guide

To become a guide, you must have the proper training and experience in the field. The amount of experience and training needed depends on the level of difficulty of the adventure you want to guide. For example, rafting guide Pat Tierney said in an interview that, when hiring for entry-level positions, he looks for candidates with enthusiasm, an interest in the outdoors (such as an education in an outdoor-related field), and completed course-work at a reputable white-water training school (there are many throughout the United States and Canada). For these positions, he is willing to hire people with no prior guiding experience other than white-water training.

The requirements for those who want to guide other kinds of extreme adventures are much more demanding. Those who wish to guide extreme adventures must have a lot of guiding experience, a great deal of safety training, and plenty of personal experience completing extreme challenges. They must have summited high mountains, climbed difficult rock faces, or navigated challenging rivers. This is also where one's personal contacts with and reputation among guide leaders (those in charge of

Anna Fortner, a white-water rafting guide on the Rogue River, pulls her raft onto the shore near Agness, Oregon, following a three-day excursion.

adventure trips) and outfitting companies (companies that set up outdoor adventures and hire guides) is very helpful, if not absolutely necessary. Guide leaders and outfitters must have complete trust in the people they hire. They have to be certain that, in intense and dangerous situations, their guides will be able to make smart decisions that will enable clients to be challenged but also to be safe. Usually, outfitting companies or guide leaders will hire someone they know personally or whom they know through others as having a solid reputation as an able and trustworthy guide.

Outdoor Education

Guides learn skills through experience and training. One place where they can get both is through participating in outdoor education programs. These programs teach participants how to be leaders in the outdoors, not just participants in an outing. There are many outdoor education programs throughout the United States and Canada; two of the most well known are Outward Bound and the National Outdoor Leadership School (NOLS). After completing courses in these programs, many graduates go on to become outdoor educators themselves, or, after additional training, instructors at the school. These are also great experiences for those who wish to become adventure guides.

Guide Certification

To call oneself a guide in the United States or Canada, one does not need to have any certification;

Students on an Outward Bound sailing ship, the *Ji Fung*, exert themselves during a sailing expedition on which they will have to learn to sail on their own, right off the coast of Sai Kung, Vietnam.

he or she is not legally required to have any formal training. Indeed, many guides have started their careers without much coursework, relying mostly on experience to learn the job. However, training and certification do ensure that a beginner guide will have at least a minimum level of guiding skills to take out in the field. Certification also shows a commitment to the career that will give both clients and employers greater confidence in the guide.

Students of NOLS link together to negotiate a stream crossing while training in the Talkeetna Mountains in Alaska. Such training gives guides the skills needed to properly guide others in wilderness situations.

In both the United States and Canada, there is only one nationally and internationally recognized organization that certifies adventure guides in skiing, mountaineering, and rock climbing: the American Mountain Guide Association (AMGA) in the United States and the Association of Canadian Mountain Guides (ACMG) in Canada. (There are numerous other guide/outdoor education schools in both countries, but none provide certification that is officially recognized nationally or internationally by other organizations or the governments of other countries. Guides who choose to get their training in this manner should choose their school wisely as the quality of instruction can vary greatly from school to school.) These organizations' certification programs are also the only in each country that are recognized by the International Federation of Mountain Guides Associations (IFMGA), an organization that exists in sixteen countries.

For those guiding river sports, there are numerous white-water schools throughout the United States and Canada, such as Whitewater Voyages in California and Chilliwack River Rafting Adventures in Alberta, Canada. These provide instruction for those who want to be river guides. But there are no organizations like the AMGA or ACMG in the river-guiding world that provide training at a guaranteed level of quality or certification that is officially recognized on a national or international level. For this reason, choosing a reputable course is very important. As with the numerous and varied mountaineering schools (outside of the AMGA and ACMG), the quality of instruction can vary greatly.

Self-Education

Education isn't limited to classes, certification programs, or experience. Guides, especially those who are new to the career, should read magazines and books about their sport. It's important to know, for example, what advances are being made in equipment and apparel, or what new accomplishments have been made by others in the sport. In addition, finding a mentor can be extremely helpful in improving one's skill level and breadth of knowledge. One should also be constantly asking questions of and carefully observing more experienced guides.

An NOLS student coils rope during a training exercise. While schools and classes are invaluable, learning from a mentor and studying on one's own are important, too.

The more information a guide has, the better he or she will be able to do the job. Continually educating oneself is an important part of being a good guide.

Pay and Job Security

Though it may be fairly simple to get a job as a guide—at least in an entry-level position—generally the pay is not very high. Guides get paid by the day, and they can make anywhere from about $40 to $180 depending on the company they work for and the difficulty of the adventure.

This pay scale may not sound too bad, but it is important to remember that guides may not work every day and that most guiding is seasonal. Because of changing weather, many outdoor adventures can take place only in a particular area during certain months of the year. This means that to work year-round, a guide must either work for a company that offers trips to places around the world, or he or she must travel to areas where guiding is in season. However, it is important to remember, as Beth Rypins points out, that guiding "is not about the money, it's about the lifestyle, the opportunities to be with and meet people and work in the outdoors." It is not a job that people take on to become rich. For most, the opportunities and experiences far outweigh the desire for a larger paycheck.

There is, however, one alternative to this situation: You could start your own guiding service. This is what Kathy Cosley and Mark Houston did. After years of working for other guiding companies, they started their own. Today, their business, Cosley and Houston Alpine Guides, is thriving.

Related Careers

For a variety of reasons, such as low pay, the difficulty of the work, and nonstop travel, most people do not guide for their entire career. So what other jobs do guides typically move on to? What other careers does guiding prepare them for? Though there is no standard career path most people take after they stop guiding, experience in the field does give a person useful tools

Experienced guides have a variety of different careers they can tackle. Working for the U.S. Forest Service, like this park ranger giving a tour of Ward Lake Trail in Alaska, is one of the many options available.

that can lead to other employment. For instance, one could become an instructor for his or her sport, or an outdoor educator for a company like the National Outdoor Leadership School. Many people are able to remain in the outdoor industry working for companies that manufacture outdoor equipment or apparel. Careers in the outdoors, such as working as a ranger or conservationist, are a possible next step. Finally, because of their experience with emergency medicine, many guides go on to work as paramedics, firefighters,

Kayak tour guide Eric Davis *(right)* gives instructions to a group of beginning kayakers on Lake Taneycomo near Branson, Missouri, as his canine companion looks on.

or emergency medical technicians (EMTs). Beyond that, there are few other careers typically related to guiding, but that doesn't mean one's experiences and skills are not useful. One simply needs to know how to apply them. Beth Rypins now uses her knowledge of kayaking and her ability to clearly inform people about the sport to host kayaking and white-water television programs. Indeed, the abilities one develops as a guide—leadership, self-reliance, determination, teamwork, and more—are helpful in just about any career. People skills are important, too. Guides learn how to work with a wide variety of people and make them feel comfortable. This is also helpful in the pursuit of just about any career.

Knowing the business of guiding is an important part of pursuing a career as an adventure tour guide. Being informed about the industry and how it operates will help lead to a successful career in the field.

The Job of Guiding

O nce one has completed the training and found a job as a guide, it's time to go to work. The opportunity to put new skills and knowledge to use, as well as the opportunity to share that expertise with clients, awaits. So what is the job of guiding all about? This chapter will discuss the experiences guides have on the job.

No Two Days Are the Same

When asked to recount a typical day as a guide, Kathryn Hess responded: "Fortunately there is no typical day . . . Every day is different. Alaska mountaineering is vastly different from [Grand] Teton

India has become a popular destination for rafting. Here, a team of kayakers maneuvers through the Zanskar River in the Himalayan region of Ladakh, which cuts deep canyons through the mountains rising up to 3,000 feet (1,000 meters).

mountaineering [in Wyoming], which is different from the Wind River Range [in the Rocky Mountains], which is very different from teaching a climbing class. The variety is what I like. Some climbs require that you get up at 2 AM, start hiking in the dark so that you are on the summit before noon (and subsequent afternoon thunderstorms) and you may not be down before dark depending on the client. Some Alaskan climbs require that you go on a night schedule so that you have frozen snow to walk on to be supported better over possible crevasses [large, deep gaps in the ice] and so that avalanches aren't as much a factor. This means that you sleep during the heat of the day and climb at night. Peaks like Denali [in Alaska; also known as Mt. McKinley; at 20,320 feet (about six kilometers), it is the highest peak in North America] take up to three weeks to climb. Normal climbing classes are easy; they start at 9 AM and ends at 4 PM. Many of the climbs in the Tetons let you spend the night at home but the climbs in Montana or the Wind River Range require that you backpack in and camp. Variety!"

Indeed, guides experience a huge variety of circumstances each time they go out on an expedition.

Clients change, terrain changes, and the weather is always shifting. Even if one is guiding the same river or the same rock face time and again, nature is unpredictable, and new opportunities and challenges are always waiting. The only expectation any guide can have of their next day on the job is the opportunity to test his or her skills and share his or her knowledge with clients. Depending on the type of guiding you are doing, however, there are some key differences between guiding experiences.

Sea kayakers paddle along the Canadian coast near the Johnstone Straits off Vancouver Island, British Columbia, one of thousands of destinations worldwide for tour guides to bring clients.

Day Trips, Multi-Day Trips, and Expeditions

One's experiences as a guide depend on the type of guiding one is doing. There are generally three levels of adventures that guides lead: day trips, multi-day trips, and expeditions. A day trip starts in the morning and finishes at the end of the same day. Typically, these trips are guided by less-experienced guides; high levels of experience and skill are generally not required. These adventures are a little more predictable than the other two, as a guide will usually take clients to the same places again and again throughout the guiding season. Often, day trips are geared toward beginning level clients, so these trips are usually not very risky or dangerous.

Multi-day trips, as the name indicates, take place over several days. These trips are led by guides who have more experience and more advanced skills than guides who lead day trips. Multi-day trips generally cover terrain that is more challenging than that of single-day trips, so the risks can be greater. Given the

How Much Is Too Much?—The Advanced Risks of Summiting 8,000-Meter Peaks

It is well known in the world of mountaineering that attempting to summit peaks above 8,000 meters high (26,229 feet, or 5 miles) poses unique risks that even the best mountaineers in the world cannot always foresee. In fact, the area above 8,000 meters is called the Death Zone because, as stated in *The Climb* by Anatoli Boukreev and G. Weston DeWalt, "elevations above 8,000 meters [are] where extended exposure to subzero temperatures and oxygen deprivation combine and kill, quickly." According to journalist Jon Krakauer in his book *Into Thin Air*, "I knew that Everest had killed more than 130 people since the British first visited the mountain in 1921—approximately one death for every four climbers who had reached the summit."

The primary reason high-altitude climbing is so dangerous is because there is very little oxygen at high elevations. Most people cannot survive in this environment without additional oxygen (which is supplied by an oxygen tank that the climber must carry on his or her back). Even with additional oxygen, both novice and experienced climbers are susceptible to severe altitude sickness. Anyone who spends time at high altitudes can

[continued on page 40]

Adventure Tour Guides: Life on Extreme Outdoor Adventures

[continued from page 39]

get high altitude cerebral edema (HACE), in which the brain swells with fluid, and high altitude pulmonary edema (HAPE), in which the lungs fill with fluid. Each of these conditions can result in death, or, at the least, leave the climber debilitated and at the mercy of his or her healthy colleagues. Though HACE is less common than HAPE, either can happen to any climber of any ability level at any time, and without warning.

Krakauer notes about HAPE (a truth that can also be stated about HACE) in *Into Thin Air*, "The only real cure . . . is rapid descent; if the victim remains at that altitude very long, death is the most likely outcome." Also of great concern at high elevations is the weather, which can change quickly and severely. And there is always potential danger from avalanches, falling rocks and ice, and hidden crevasses (large, deep gaps in the ice), among others.

For many, this begs the question: Should guides take clients into such an environment? Indeed, in *The Climb*, Boukreev noted his uncertainty about just that: "It is with great reservation that I work to bring inexperienced men and women in this world [of high-altitude mountaineering]." Regardless of the answer to this question, the reality remains: As long as there are people who wish to push the limits of the human mind and body, there will be a demand for people to guide them there, even when the risks are extraordinarily high.

additional time, the adventurers can also travel to more remote areas. The group must be completely self-reliant because it is often difficult to get outside help. Weather can also play an important role on multi-day trips.

The most challenging kind of adventure guiding is expedition guiding. Expeditions are trips taken to very remote locations around the world to attempt difficult challenges, such as summiting a tall mountain, navigating a raging river, or scaling a sheer rock face. These trips are open only to clients who have considerable outdoor experience, and they are led by experienced guides of the highest caliber. These trips may take months to complete. They put everyone in the most extreme circumstances nature has to offer. There is little room for even the smallest error. The best guides in the world have suffered injuries, frostbite, and even death on expeditions of this level. But these are also the adventures that offer the greatest rewards.

Common Experiences

Two days of guiding are never the same. Leading a day or multi-day trip differs enormously from leading an

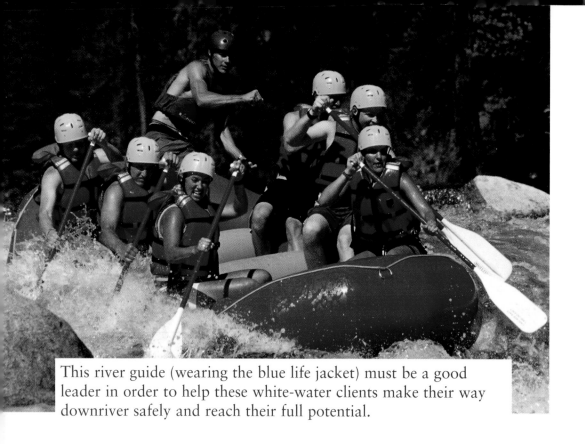

This river guide (wearing the blue life jacket) must be a good leader in order to help these white-water clients make their way downriver safely and reach their full potential.

expedition. But there are some common experiences that all guides can relate to.

Being a Leader

All guides are leaders. At every level, others are relying on them to show the way through a challenging situation. Guides must make decisions quickly and enforce them. They must trust themselves and be trustworthy. All guides experience the joys and fears of being responsible for the welfare of others.

Outdoor Living

Guiding is done outdoors. All guides have the privilege of experiencing the outdoors on a daily basis. As a guide, one gets to be "outdoors with friends," stated Beth Rypins. "You are in a beautiful, fun environment."

Intimacy of Challenge

One of the primary joys of outdoor guiding is taking clients to the limits of their abilities and helping them succeed. The challenges people face on an outdoor adventure expose them to new and unique parts of their personalities. "We [get] to share these intimate experiences," noted Rypins. "Being in situations that are difficult and challenging for people, that require people to go beyond their comfort levels [puts them in a place where] they really get to see what they are made of as human beings."

Doing the Job

The daily experiences of adventure guiding are always changing. Nature and new clients guarantee that no two trips are the same. Doing the job of guiding continually provides new opportunities and challenges. Regardless of the kind of sport or level of the adventure, all guides experience the joys and frustrations of leadership, outdoor living, and sharing adventures with new people.

Life as an Adventure Guide

4

Adventure guides lead uniquely challenging and rewarding lives. They are continually pushing their limits, both physically and mentally. Guides travel regularly. And they take responsibility for others' lives in the most unforgiving places on earth: the extreme and remote outdoors. It is a rigorous life, but a life that feeds a deep passion.

The life of a guide is very fulfilling, but it also has its difficulties. It's dangerous, seasonal work. Clients can be as interesting and kind as they can be rude and inconsiderate. The pay is low, but the experiences are second to none. In this chapter, we will explore some of the upsides and downsides to life as an adventure guide.

The Clients

Guides are "exposed to parts of society that [they] would have never been exposed to," said Rypins. Adventure guides get the opportunity to meet and get to know people from all walks of life. In the outdoors, people are removed from their everyday lives. Notes Rypins, "In that [outdoor] environment it's not what you do, it's who you are." One's identity as a doctor, lawyer, or engineer, and his or her position in society, becomes irrelevant. Rypins added: "[Guiding] allowed me to see humanity and be exposed to people on all levels, and I enjoyed that. It was a privilege to be with people in that way."

Working with clients also gives guides the unique opportunity to help people overcome their own physical or psychological limitations and have extraordinary experiences. "People consistently had these mini-awakenings in their lives because it was so meaningful for them to be in these exquisitely beautiful places on this very demanding river," said Rypins. When asked what she likes about guiding,

An adventure guide takes a well-deserved dip in a stream. Being able to enjoy the outdoors every day is one of the attractions to the job and lifestyle of guiding.

Kathryn Hess said, among other things, "I like helping people overcome fears and succeed at things they didn't know they could."

On the other hand, clients are not always fun to work with. As a guide, you are in effect working for your clients, and some may treat you like a servant. "I don't like super high-maintenance clients who think of you as their personal slave," Hess noted. Dealing with difficult people is one of the unpleasant realities of a career as an adventure guide.

The Risks and Rewards of Outdoor Life

Living in the beauty of nature and testing one's mind and body regularly are privileges few people have the opportunity to experience, let alone make a living at. "I love the challenge of getting to the top of something and then the views that follow," said Hess. The physical demands of guiding ensure that guides stay in excellent physical shape. Adventure guiding promotes a healthy lifestyle in a variety of spectacular environments.

But guides must regularly face great risks posed by living in the outdoors. The rigors of anticipating risks, enduring bad weather, and lacking everyday conveniences can take their toll. There have been many accidents that have left guides and clients alike injured, frostbitten, and even dead. Guides must be healthy in order to do the job. Illness or injury can leave them unemployed.

The Life of a Guide:
A Profile of Beth Rypins

Beth Rypins started river raft guiding when she was sixteen years old. Growing up in San Francisco, California, she happened upon her future career by chance. She went on to become a world class white-water kayaker and one of the most respected white-water rafting guides in the world. This is her story:

"As a teenager I was an inner-city kid on drugs going nowhere fast. I got a job cooking at a kayak school, where I learned to paddle in exchange for work, and I saw people on the river, guiding rafts. I didn't know what the job required, but I knew they were working in a great environment that I wanted to be a part of. I went to a one-week white-water school where, supposedly, you learn everything you need to know to become a commercial guide. I started guiding in 1980, which was a drought year in California. The low water was slow moving and I had plenty of opportunities to learn. Nonetheless I was in way over my head; thankfully no one got hurt. I was very eager to learn, read everything I could, talked to everyone I met, [and] asked a million questions. This is how I improved my skills and learned how to be a better river guide. My commitment was to be the very best kayaker and raft guide I could possibly be. I have now been guiding for twenty-two years.

[continued on page 50]

[continued from page 49]

"Rivers have provided me with a good learning environment. They've carried me all over the world and exposed me to different cultures and languages. And, through guiding, I've grown up as a person. I've learned to make decisions that keep people safe, and to take responsibility for people in situations where they can't take responsibility for themselves.

"But nobody excels alone. There have been many people who have helped me along the way. And it has been through working with others that I have been able to accomplish many of my goals. In particular, I worked with a tight-knit team of guides, and we came to depend on ourselves and each other with great fluidity.

"In the end the river has given me confidence, and guiding has shaped my personality. Guiding has been a satisfying and fulfilling career."

The Freedom, and Instability, of Seasonal Work

Guides are constantly on the move. In order to work full-time, they must travel because, as has been noted, guiding is seasonal work. In any given area, because of changing weather, guiding can take place

Adventure tour guides can specialize in a great variety of physical activities. Here, a group rides down a country road as part of the Pack and Paddle Adventure Bike Tour.

only during certain months of the year. Once the season is over, a guide must go where work is available. Also, many of the adventures that guides lead are in remote areas of the world. This constant travel means that "you don't live anywhere," said Rypins. Yes, most guides have a home base, but they are often not there. The experiences of traveling the world and exploring remote locations are some of the great benefits of being an adventure guide. However, the lack of a stable home life and

One of the rewards of guiding is being able to engage with people on a very personal level. Here, client Mark van Alstine *(left)* takes a breather with his tour guide, Subash Tamang, at their camp near Ladakh, India.

the fatigue caused by constantly being on the move can be tough.

The seasonal nature of guiding gives guides a lot of freedom. They are not confined to a set schedule, and their environment is constantly changing. But this freedom does come at a price. Guides usually aren't paid well, and most don't get the benefits of job security or health insurance offered by many typical full-time jobs.

At the End of the Day

"Guiding gave me confidence in life," summed up Beth Rypins. Indeed, the intensity of working as a guide demands that one be able to operate effectively in various and tough situations. Faced with taking others into the extreme challenges presented by the outdoors, those who guide adventures develop the ability to deal with any and all of the challenges life sets forth.

Glossary

avalanche A large mass of ice, rocks, or other material that moves quickly down a mountainside.

client In the adventure guide business, a person who pays a guide to be taken on an adventure.

conservationist One who works to conserve or protect nature.

CPR Cardiopulmonary resuscitation; a combination of chest compressions and mouth-to-mouth breathing used to resuscitate a person who has stopped breathing.

crevasse A large, deep crack in the ice.

expedition In adventure guiding, an adventure of the highest, most challenging level.

frostbite The partial freezing of a part of the body; injury to a body part due to freezing temperatures.

high altitude cerebral edema (HACE) A condition that people contract at high altitudes in which the brain fills with fluid and swells.

high altitude pulmonary edema (HAPE) A condition in which the lungs fill up with fluid as a result of the body adapting to high elevation.

mentor Someone who teaches or coaches a person who is less experienced.

mountaineering The sport of climbing mountains.

outfitter A company that arranges guided adventures.

strenuous Characterized as being very difficult or physically demanding.

summit The highest point.

For More Information

American Alpine Institute
1515 12th Street
Bellingham, WA 98225
(360) 671-1505
Web site: http://www.mtnguide.com

American Mountain Guides Association (AMGA)
710 Tenth Street, Suite 101
Golden, CO 80401
(303) 271-0984
Web site: http://www.amga.com

American River Touring Association
24000 Casa Loma Road
Groveland, CA 95321
(800) 323-2782
Web site: http://www.arta.org

National Outdoor Leadership
    School (NOLS)
284 Lincoln Street
Lander, WY 82520-2848
(307) 332-5300
Web site: http://www.nols.edu

Outward Bound
100 Mystery Point Road
Garrison, NY 10524-9757
(845) 424-4000
Web site: http://www.outwardbound.org

United States Mountain Guides
    Association (USMGA)
P.O. Box 267
Intervale, NH 03845
Web site: http://www.usmga.net

Whitewater Voyages
5225 San Pablo Dam Road
El Sobrante, CA 94805
(800) 400-RAFT (7238)
Web site: http://www.whitewatervoyages.com

Wilderness Medical Associates
189 Dudley Road
Bryant Pond, ME 04219
(207) 665-2707
Web site: http://www.wildmed.com

In Canada

Alpine Club of Canada
Indian Flats Road
P.O. Box 8040
Canmore, AB T1W 2T8
(403) 678-3200
Web site: http://www.alpineclubofcanada.ca

Association of Canadian Mountain Guides (ACMG)
Box 8341
Canmore, AB T1W 2V1
(403) 678-2885
Web site: http://www.acmg.ca

Web Sites

Due to the changing nature of Internet links, the Rosen Publishing Group, Inc., has developed an on-line list of Web sites related to the subject of this book. This site is updated regularly. Please use this link to access the list:

http://www.rosenlinks.com/ec/adtg/

For Further Reading

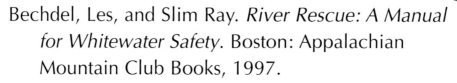

Bechdel, Les, and Slim Ray. *River Rescue: A Manual for Whitewater Safety*. Boston: Appalachian Mountain Club Books, 1997.

Bennett, Jeff. *The Essential Whitewater Kayaker: A Complete Course*. Camden, ME : Ragged Mountain Press, 1999.

Graydon, Don, and Kurt Hanson, eds. *Mountaineering: The Freedom of the Hills*. Seattle: The Mountaineers, 1997.

Lull, John. *Sea Kayaking: Safety and Rescue*. Berkeley, CA: Wilderness Press, 2001.

Selters, Andrew. *Glacier Travel and Crevasse Rescue*. Seattle: The Mountaineers, 1999.

Bibliography

American Alpine Institute. Retrieved March 2002 (http://www.aai.cc).

Boukreev, Anatoli, and G. Weston DeWalt. *The Climb: Tragic Ambitions on Everest.* New York: St. Martin's Press, 1997.

Cosley and Houston Alpine Guides. Retrieved March 2002 (http://www.cosleyhouston.com).

Krakauer, Jon. *Into Thin Air: A Personal Account of the Mount Everest Disaster.* New York: Villard, 1998.

Wilderness Medical Associates. Retrieved March 2002 (http:// www.wildmed.com).

Index

About the Author

Chérie Turner is a writer and editor who lives in San Francisco, California.

Acknowledgments

My deepest thanks go out to Beth Rypins for her friendship, support, and continual willingness to share her expertise and advice. Thank you also to Timmy Sullivan for his thoughts, friendship, and enthusiastic support. And thank you to Dr. Pat Tierney at Adrift Adventures, Kathryn Hess at Jackson Hole Mountain Guides, Tom Clausing at Rescue Specialists, and Kathy Cosley of Cosley and Houston Alpine Guides for sharing their experience, knowledge, and expertise.

Photo Credits

Cover, p. 47 © Layne Kennedy/Corbis; p. 5 © Lucido Studio, Inc./ Corbis; p. 8 © Ken Redding/Corbis; p. 10 © Roy Morsch/Corbis; p. 12 © Richard T. Nowitz/Corbis; p. 15 © Chris Rainer/Corbis; pp. 19, 26, 29, 37 © Joel W. Rogers/Corbis; pp. 23, 32, 35 © AP/Wide World Photos; p. 25 © Michael S. Yamashita; p. 31 © Bob Rowan; Progressive Image/Corbis; p. 42 © David Stoecklein/Corbis; p. 51 © Philip Gould/Corbis; p. 52 © David Samuel Robbins/Corbis.

Series Design

Les Kanturek

Layout

Tahara Hasan

Editor

Eliza Berkowitz